# Confident?

[-adj, Feeling or show-
ing confidence.]

## Confidence

[-n, firm trust; feeling of reliance
or certainty; boldness.]

ISBN 978-0-9564512-0-0

Edited by Ray Goudie

Design of this episode by Peter C. Series design by Helen Martin.

Cover and interior illustrations by Charlotte Cooke

Published by New Generation Music.
Caedmon Complex, Bristol Road, Thornbury,
Bristol, BS35 3JA, UK. www.ngm.org.uk

Printed in Great Britain by the MPG Books Group,
Bodmin and King's Lynn

Unless otherwise stated biblical quotations are taken from
The Holy Bible, New International Version, Copyright
© 1973, 1978, 1984 International Bible Society, used
by permission of Zondervan Bible Publishers.

* Scripture taken from the New King James Version. Copyright ©
1982 by Thomas Nelson, Inc. Used by permission. All rights reserved.

**Mixed Sources**

Product group from well-managed
forests, controlled sources and
recycled wood or fiber
www.fsc.org  Cert no. TT-COC-002303
© 1996 Forest Stewardship Council

FSC

# Preface

**T**his book is for anyone like me who sometimes swings from being confident to feeling a failure. It's a book full of encouragement, wise words, poems, songs and stories to lift your spirit and get you back on your feet again ready to face life once more.

It's a book you can pick up when life is good and when life hits you hard. When others pull you down and criticise you or when you are your worst critic, pick up this book and flick to any section and 'eat' some encouraging words, even have a little laugh at yourself! It could make a real difference to each day of your life.

Through these pages you will feel accepted, really loved and realise afresh how amazing you are! Leave a copy by your bed, in the lounge, in your bag or briefcase or even in your bathroom! Take it with you wherever you go, read a few pages and become that confident person you are meant to be.

My desire is that your hope will be renewed and your confidence will soar!

On what

are you

## basing your

# confidence?

Some trust in chariots
and some in horses,
but we trust
in the name of the
Lord our God.

Trust

[ -n, firm belief in the reliability,
truth, or strength of a person or
thing. ]

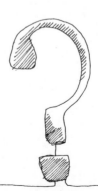

**P**eople look at me standing on a stage speaking to hundreds and sometimes thousands of people and think I am a very confident person. However, the truth is that on one of my very first times on a stage, I somehow managed to fall off it!

It was the opening night of a presentation called 'Time for Christmas'. I was in a contemporary choir/band called Unity and although I went on to sing in the band, at this point I was one of the narrators. Imagine the scene, the curtains open and there on the side of the stage were two narrators sitting on chairs. The spotlight shines on us and my friend, Frances, starts to speak her lines. At that point, I decided to cross my legs. Unknown to me, one of the legs of my chair was off the stage and therefore when I crossed my legs, promptly I and my chair fell from the stage much to the amusement of the whole audience!

Even years later, if anyone had asked me to speak from stage, I would have been incredibly nervous unless it had been scripted for me. I was happy being a singer at least that is what I told everyone else. Secretly, I always wanted to be a public speaker but never felt I had the confidence to fulfil that dream. I wouldn't even tell my closest friend my secret desire in case I would be laughed at! Despite the fact that I had been trained to speak in public and am, in fact, qualified to teach elocution, I still did not have the confidence to face an audience. Interestingly, I have since discovered that statistics tells us the main fear we have as human beings is the fear of speaking in public, so I was not alone! How did I overcome that fear? By firstly sharing my dream with my husband and believing him when he said I could do it and secondly confronting my fear and taking the opportunities that came my way.

# Food for thought

A man was waiting at the train station for his train to arrive when it was announced that the train would be late, so he decided to get a coffee and some biscuits. He sat down with his coffee and newspaper and began to read. At the same time another man sat down at his table with his coffee in hand too. After a few minutes, the first man decided to open his packet of four biscuits. He took one and left the rest on the table and went back to reading his newspaper. However, out of the corner of his eye, he saw the other man lean over and also take one of the biscuits from the pack. He could not believe it; the man had just helped himself to *his* biscuits! He thought to himself, 'Well, maybe he's hungry'. A few minutes later he took another biscuit from the pack and pulled the biscuits from the middle of the table and placed them close to his coffee cup. A couple of minutes went by, then the second man again leaned over and took the last biscuit from the pack. The first man was really annoyed, but before he could say anything he noticed his train had arrived at the station. As he boarded the train he thought to himself, 'What a nerve! I can't believe that man had the confidence just to lean over and steal my biscuits from under my nose!' Later when the ticket collector asked him for his ticket, he put his hand in his pocket and discovered not only his train ticket but also his packet of biscuits!

Who was more confident? The one who really owned the biscuits or the one who thought he did? Both displayed full confidence thinking they knew the truth, but only one had the real truth!

# Step by step

In my early years the church I attended in Ayr in Scotland was very unusual in that although men were encouraged to pray publicly I never was because I was female. Women were not allowed to speak publicly in our church. Therefore, when I joined an organisation called British Youth for Christ a number of years later, I was petrified at first that someone would ask me to pray out loud. A year or so later, I was asked to pray the opening prayer at an annual national conference. I had been growing in confidence in praying in small prayer meetings but I felt this was way out of my league. It was made worse by some kind soul telling me that I would be the first woman ever to pray publicly in the history of this yearly conference! That really added to my confidence!

I was awake the whole night, going over and over my prayer. I was praying about praying! It would have been hilarious had I not been so scared. I reminded myself that I was talking to God and not to 400 evangelists, but still I could not stop shaking! My prayer lasted about 30 seconds and I am not sure to this day whether people heard my beating heart louder than they heard my prayer. Today I never think twice about praying out loud, so what has happened? I overcame my fear by trusting God with each new opportunity. Now I spend a lot of my time encouraging others to do the same!

Heb 13:6

So we say with **confidence**, the Lord is my helper, I will not be afraid.

# You are my precious diamond

My joy in you knows no bounds. My heart sings with delight at who you are. What beauty you display! My favour falls on you and my grace covers you. I adore you and I always will do. You are like a diamond, a precious and rare diamond. You are worth more than you could ever know. You shine, sparkle, gleam and shed your beauty and wonderful fragrance far and near. I will always love and adore you and will never fail you. You can have complete faith and confidence in me.

The essence of faith and trust is to be convinced of the reliability of God.

# Waterfall

*Oh my heart cries out for you*
*All my hunger breaking*
*    through*
*Pure obsession drives within*
*Oh Jesus you're my everything*

*Your desire is my command*
*Let me drink from your*
*    own hand*
*Oh the thirst that*
*    grips my soul*
*Oh Jesus you are*
*    beautiful*

*Here is where you*
*    will find me*
*Underneath*
*    your waterfall*
*Desperate for your presence*
*Let your Spirit fall*
*Under the waterfall*

*Fill me, soak me through and through*
*No longer I 'til only you*
*Cleanse me, heal me with your love*
*Living water from above*

## Under God's waterfall is where we are drenched in confidence

Lyrics by Ray Goudie, 2008.  Song by Ray Goudie; Dan Goudie; Neil Wilson
© Published by ngm/Daybreak music/Fierce! Publishing

# How is this for confidence?

Though my father and mother forsake me the Lord will receive me!

Ps 27:10

You will never be forsaken!

# Miracle in the Snow

"Mum, Mum look! It's snowing outside", said my eleven year old son with huge excitement. He had just realised that he probably would not be going to school that day and therefore could not contain his excitement. As I turned to look out of the window, I could not believe what I was seeing. The sky was heavy with snow; the snowflakes were falling fast and there was more than a foot of snow outside our house. I turned on the news to hear the words, 'We have had more snow than anticipated with Bristol being the worse hit place. Bristol airport has been closed and the buses are not running. Our advice is that you do not travel unless you really need to.'

It was Friday, the morning of my Spiritual Health Conference in Bristol and I had around 400 women travelling to Bristol from various parts of the country! You can imagine my thoughts at that point! Am I going to have a conference? Is everyone going to have the confidence to travel through the snow? Even if they want to come, are they going to be physically able to get here? What about me and my team? Are we going to be able to get out of our homes? Lord, HELP!

My confidence was not very high at that point, but the question was 'on what was I basing my confidence?' I knew my confidence had to be in God and not on the weather and news reports I was hearing on the television. According to the media reports this conference was not going to happen!

Ray and I started to pray and ask God what he was saying. Ray got a clear picture of Jesus being in the boat with us and telling us that we would all get to the other side. So, we put our faith in God's word and despite all the circumstances around us, we confidently went ahead with all the plans for the conference. Even when we could not get our car out of our drive we just made other plans. Someone in ngm (new generation music – the charity organisation Ray and I lead) had a four wheel drive car and therefore was able to drive through the deep snow and pick us up.

I called a friend of mine from Scotland who was travelling with a group of people to the conference that morning to discover they were stuck in Glasgow. Their flight to Bristol had been cancelled. She told me she had been offered another flight and asked me, "Nancy, where is Gatwick?"

I gasped and said, "Lesley, Gatwick is the other side of the country from Bristol! You would have to take a train from there to Reading, change at Reading and then take a train from there to Bristol!" She told me, "We will do it! We have to be there Nancy!"

Another lady who was snowed in called a taxi but had to walk through the snow with all her luggage to the main road as the taxi could not get down her street. Another lady emailed me to tell me that it would take more than snow to keep her away. With these encouraging remarks, my confidence in God was growing all the time. Our trucks and vans had travelled very early in the morning through all the snow to be there. It took them much longer than it would have normally, but they had made it and were at that point setting up.

The media throughout the morning kept on telling us how difficult it was to travel and were showing how the roads were thick with snow. There were so many voices proclaiming gloom and doom! We kept reminding ourselves that our confidence was not in the media but our confidence was in our God and in his words. When people arrived, there were many stories of how against all the odds people had made it to the conference. They had been determined to come and God had made it possible. At the end of the day, only four people did not make it to the conference because of the snow. Everyone else made it to the other side. Praise God! It's amazing what can happen when we place our confidence in God and his promises. For us it could have been a complete disaster, but instead as we trusted in God what we saw was miraculous!

No matter what you are going through, place your confidence in God and his word for you for he is the God of miracles!

# The one who calls you is faithful and he will do it.

*Praise be to the Lord, to God our Saviour who daily bears our burdens.*

Psalm 68:19

It is wonderfully releasing to know the truth that God daily bears our burdens.

Whatever is concerning you, whatever is worry-ing you, or stressing you, believe the fact that God is with you and is carrying each burden for you. There is no need for you to carry it too.

*Have no fear of sudden disaster..... for the Lord will be your **confidence** and will keep your foot from being snared.*

Prov 3:25-26

# Through the eyes of God

In all aspects of life, it is important to see yourself as
God sees you! Ask him how he sees you. I am sure you
will be surprised and encouraged at his response.

You are my beautiful
creation; my outrageous-
ly amazing child. You
fill my heart with much
joy and my feet cannot
stop dancing. I rejoice
over you constantly!

*The Lord your God is with you, he is mighty to save.*
*He will take great delight in you, he will quiet you*
*with his love, he will rejoice over you with singing!*

Zeph 3:17

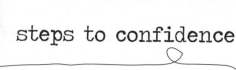

# steps to confidence

The fruit of righteousness
will be peace; the effect of
righteousness will be quietness and **confidence** forever.

Isaiah 32:17

Blessed is the one who trusts in the
Lord, whose **confidence** is in him.
He will be like a tree
planted by the water
that sends out its
roots by the stream.
It does not fear when
heat comes; its leaves
are always green.
It has no worries in a year of
drought and never fails to bear
fruit.

Jer 17:7-8

In him and through faith
in him we may approach
God with freedom and
**confidence**.

Eph 3:12

Let us then approach the throne of grace with **confidence**, so that we may receive mercy and find grace to help us in our time of need.

Heb 4:16

So do not throw away your **confidence**; it will be richly rewarded.

Heb 10:35

Though an army besiege me, my heart will not fear; though war break out against me, even then will I be **confident**.

Ps 27:3

I am still **confident** of this; I will see the goodness of the Lord in the land of the living. Wait for the Lord; be strong and take heart and wait for the Lord.

Ps 27:13-14

# You Are Very Good

Come with me back before time began; when empty darkness covered the face of the earth. The earth was a shapeless, chaotic mess, formless and empty. Breaking into this dark, shapeless, formless mess comes the Word. Like a sharp blade cutting through ice, the Word speaks, "Let there be light" and light appears. The light and darkness took it in turn to rule and together they formed the first day.

And the Word was delighted and rejoiced
in what he had made and said

## "This is good."

The Word again spoke "Let the vapours separate to form the sky above and the oceans below." And it was so!

The Word observed what He had made and said

## "This is good!"

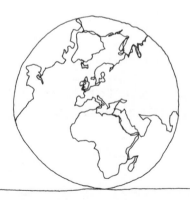

The Word spoke to the waters "Give way. Be gathered into one place and let the earth be seen." Then the Word spoke to the earth, "Produce vegetation, trees, grass, plants and fruit of all kinds."

And it happened just as He said. And the Word looked and said

"This is good."

The Word spoke "Let bright lights appear in the sky to give light to the earth and to identify day and night." The Word made the sun, the moon, and the stars to give light on the earth.

And the Word was pleased with what He made and said

"This is good."

The Word spoke to the waters to produce fish and all kinds of living creatures and it was so. The Word spoke and the skies were filled with birds of every kind. The Word looked at them with pleasure, blessed them and told them "Multiply, let your numbers increase; fill the earth."

And the Word said

"This is good."

The Word spoke and the land produced every kind of animal, cattle, reptiles, wild creatures, wildlife of every kind.

The Word saw what He had made and said

"This is good."

"The Word then said, "Let mankind be made in the image of God to rule over the earth, the skies and the seas. So the Word created male and female in the image of Himself. The Word breathed into mankind the breath of life and blessed them. "Be fruitful and increase in number; fill the earth, rule over the fish of the seas, the birds of the skies and every living creature that moves."

The Word looked and danced and rejoiced in what He had made and said

## "This is very good."

Now hear the word of God speak deep into your own heart. As God looks at you he says, **'You are very good. You are special in my sight. I have made you in my image and I am pleased with what I have made!'**

Open up your heart and allow God's word to pen-
etrate your whole being as God says to you

# "You are very good."

# My Joy in You

You are so beautiful; you fill my mouth with singing and my heart with much joy. I created you as you are; a person with great value and talents. You have gifts beyond what you can see and comprehend at this time. Come my precious one, come and live in all I have for you. My joy in you is constant and will never end.

# Know before you go

**R**ay and I had been treated to a wonderful couple of days in Paris. During our visit, someone recommended a restaurant to us and told us it was a very special place.

As we walked in through the door of the restaurant, however, we were warmly greeted by the Head Waiter who took one look at Ray and promptly strongly suggested that he should wear a tie. He gave Ray a huge and very ugly tie to wear. There was no room for negotiation! Ray apologised and said if he had known that a tie was obligatory then he would have worn one. I started to giggle as I saw my trendy husband trying to make this old fashioned tie look reasonable on him.

When Ray looked suitably attired we were then shown into this amazing dining area. The atmosphere was wonderful and the tables were arranged around a dance floor. On stage a saxophonist was performing. The building itself was stunning and it felt as though we had been transported back to the 1930s. As we sat down at our designated table, I began to wonder just how much this evening was likely to cost, but before my thoughts turned into worries the saxophonist approached our table. She was an outstanding musician and Ray and I began to relax and enjoy the music.

Before too long, the waiter presented us with two menus, one for me and one for Ray. I looked at mine and thought there is something strange about this menu, but I couldn't quite figure out what it was. Then it dawned on me! There were no prices on the menu. I panicked! I whispered my predicament to Ray. He looked puzzled and told me all the prices were on his menu! It became obvious that there was one menu for the women with no prices and one for the men with prices. I suddenly felt completely insecure! I told Ray I could not order my food without knowing how much it cost. It was also obvious that we could not swop menus as the waiter was standing near our table. So, in whispers Ray explained that each course would almost need an extra mortgage on our house!

It wasn't quite as bad as that, but we were kicking ourselves that we hadn't previously asked how much a meal would cost – what a mistake! We contemplated walking out but realised that would be even more embarrassing! We decided to inwardly pray, trust God and choose the cheapest thing on the menu. Fortunately, the cheapest main course was something we both liked and included a pudding. We had the most amazing night which will remain in our memories forever, however never again will we make that mistake!

Confidence grows in a place of security and ~~disappears~~ rapidly in a place of insecurity!

# Be a confidence booster

"Nancy, I think you should write a book!"

The words hung in the air! I looked at my husband's face and expected him to burst out laughing any minute, but the laughter never came. When he saw my bewildered look he said, "I'm serious, Nancy, I really think you should write a book about your spiritual health plans." I was shocked! I had been writing spiritual health plans (a bit like a physical health and diet plan, except for your spiritual health) for people to work through and they had been producing amazing results in people's lives. Nevertheless, I was still shocked when Ray suggested it. I was embarrassed when he later mentioned it to a publisher in London and fully expected the man to laugh, instead, he was very enthusiastic. I came home with a contract for at least one book.

Ray's words gave me the confidence to start writing and I am so glad he did. As I started my first book I discovered a real love and passion for writing. I so enjoy the creativity in writing and seeing how lives can be changed through simple words and stories. I know that if Ray had not encouraged me, my first book would never have been written. He gave me confidence to go for it even though he says he could never write a book himself. It's so important to surround ourselves with people whose words build our confidence.

*I can do everything through him
who gives me strength.*

Phil 4:13

(For Spiritual Health Plans – please see 'Nancy Goudie's Spiritual Health Workout' book – available on www.nancygoudie.com, www.amazon.co.uk or www.ngm.org.uk)

# Don't be a confidence destroyer

I t was Christmas Eve and our band had been asked to appear on Scottish television. It was a live show and although we were excited we were also very nervous as this was our first time on the box. The television people told us where to stand and in which direction to face for the cameras. In our shows I usually stood in a certain place, but I was moved and told to stand where another girl usually stood and she was told to stand in my place. When we saw the show later, people noticed that the cameras had picked me out several times, but I never really thought much about it. The day had been fun and we all really enjoyed ourselves.

However, the husband of the girl who would normally have stood where I stood obviously had a problem. It got back to me that he was annoyed that I had swopped places with his wife and he said that if his wife had been standing there, then she would have been the one who was highlighted on television and not me. He also complained that I was not a great singer and said I sang out of tune. He complained, "The McVicars' (my maiden name – he was meaning me and my three brothers) are all full of confidence but have no talent." His words were devastating and caused me much pain. The little confidence I had was wrecked completely. I know he was talking out of insecurity and possibly jealousy and probably didn't realise his words were cruel, but it was a real reminder of how all of us need to be careful of what we say. Words can so easily destroy!

Proverbs 12:18

Reckless words pierce like a sword, but the tongue of the wise brings healing

# Forest Fire

**L**et me paint a picture in your mind. In your imagination, begin to see a huge forest of strong and well-developed trees. You long to go and explore all the ancient paths which crisscross throughout this forest, but before you can do so you notice a woman walking by. As you watch her, she lights up a cigarette and carelessly throws away the match. Unknown to her that small match is still burning and because the forest is so dry, it isn't long before a fire starts. Before you can shout for help the small fire grows and grows and suddenly is out of control. You stand back in horror as the flames cause total destruction. Minutes before, you were looking at creativity and beauty at its highest level, now all you can see is a huge ball of fire as it devours everything in sight. Your heart is filled with sadness at the destruction around you.

The picture then changes! Begin to see yourself looking at the forest long after the fire has been put out. You walk through the charred and black remains disturbed in your spirit about the waste of life. All the trees and their beauty have been burned and destroyed. All around you is death and destruction. As you stand appalled at the waste of life you notice at various points in the soil that someone has come and planted new young trees alongside the dead ones. Someone has planted shrubs and flowers in the midst of decay. Already these young trees are beginning to grow and these plants are beginning to take root. Your heart is suddenly revived as you see that out of a desolate situation, life is prevailing. You rejoice in the life you see and know that if you were to come back to this land many years from now the scene would once again be teeming with life.

In the Bible it says 'The tongue is a small part of the body yet it can make great boasts. A great forest can be set on fire by a small spark. The tongue can be that small spark bringing destruction and corruption to all around.'

At various points in our lives, careless words spoken to you can be like a tiny spark of destruction thrown into your heart. Some words can cause a huge fire deep within you and may even leave you feeling destroyed. However, just as that forest can be renewed and refreshed so can your heart, spirit, soul and body be made new again. Speak to your spirit and plant wise and healing words within you. Plant words such as 'I am not a mistake.' 'I am loved.' 'I am special.' 'There is nothing I cannot do.' 'There is no one quite like me.' Continue to plant positive words within you each day and soon you will see them taking root. Plant good, wise and healing words and so like that forest, you will begin to feel strong and whole again. An old proverb says

'Words can kill. Words give life. They are either poison or fruit – you choose.'

# Watch our words!

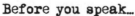

**Before you speak...**

is it True?

is it Helpful?

is it Instructive?

is it Necessary?

is it Kind?

*Whatever is true, whatever is noble, whatever is right, whatever is pure, whatever is lovely, whatever is admirable – if anything is excellent or praiseworthy, think about such things ... and the God of peace will be with you!*

Phil 4:8-9

# Change our thinking - change our ways

I magine the scene, it was in the 80's and the band Ray and I were in, called Heartbeat, was in the middle of a concert. In the venue were hundreds of teenagers who had seen us in their school that week. They had enjoyed what we did and had come to see us perform at the local theatre. The band was loud but it seemed like the audience were even louder at times as they whistled and cheered through the songs. In the middle of the set, we had asked Dorry, one of our singers, to perform a beautiful slow ballad. She had an amazing voice and really suited this type of song. She hadn't been sure about performing this song to this audience, but Ray and I persuaded her that the audience would love it. The audience grew quiet as the song progressed and then one girl who was standing right at the front of the stage turned to her friend and shouted, "This is a boring song!" I am sure the comment didn't do much to increase Dorry's confidence, but later both she and the rest of the band howled with laughter.

I'm sure the girl did not mean us to hear her comment, nor did she mean any harm by it, she just spoke (or shouted, I should say) her mind!

Always be careful of what you say! In this instance the comments were taken with a laugh; in fact we still laugh at this situation even today, but sometimes the words that come from our mouths can cause insecurity in others.

# A Father's Love

God shields you and cares
for you; he guards you as
the apple of his eye!

Deut 32:10b

# The Naked Truth

I n the 80's my husband Ray and I used to travel extensively throughout Britain and Europe with our band. In those days when we visited an area the organiser would often arrange for us to stay in people's homes rather than put us in a hotel. The people who gave us hospitality were often people we had never met before.

One evening, two of our band who are married arrived at their host's house and throughout the hour or so before going to bed received instructions about the morning. The hosts very kindly told our fellow musicians that they should treat the house as though it was their own and told them to help themselves to breakfast the following morning as they would be leaving very early.

In the morning when our friends heard their hosts leave the house, the husband decided to go to the kitchen to get some breakfast. As he usually slept with nothing on and as his host had encouraged him to treat the house like his own, he went downstairs into the kitchen naked. He was getting breakfast ready to take upstairs when he heard the front door being opened with a key. As you can imagine, he panicked! His confidence at walking around the house with nothing on suddenly disappeared! He ran into the walk-in larder and closed the door and prayed like crazy that the host would not open the larder door. Fortunately the host only came back for something he had forgotten and then left!

This funny incident shows that our friend's confidence was fuelled by his knowledge of the truth, but when that was challenged his confidence flew out of the window or in this case, into the walk-in larder! To my knowledge he never did that again!

# Questions?

**Do you always fear the worst?**
*I'm going to fail!*
*Bad things always happen to me!*

**Do you constantly use 'never' or 'always'?**
*I will never make the grade!*
*I always get bad results.*

**Are you always putting yourself down?**
*I'm no good!*
*I am such a failure!*

**Are you a people pleaser?**
*I always say yes when really I should say no.*

**Are you able to accept compliments?**
*Oh, I wasn't very good.*
*I didn't do very well.*
*Anyone could have done what I did.*

YOU ARE SPECIAL

YOU ARE CHOSEN

GOD'S CHILD

YOU ARE LOVED BEYOND ALL MEASURE

THERE IS NOTHING YOU AND GOD CANNOT DO TOGETHER

# CONFIDENT?

**W**e often think others have more confidence than we do, but the truth is that we all struggle with confidence from time to time.

When my husband Ray said his first words on stage he got it all wrong. All he had to say was "Hello, I am Ray from Prestwick." However, because he was very nervous what came out was "Hello, I'm Prestwick from Ray!" When you are lacking in confidence sometimes words just don't come out the way they should!

A number of years later one of our band who had not spoken much from stage went to the microphone and said, "God has told me that there is someone here tonight who is deaf in both eyes and God wants to heal you. So if you are deaf in both eyes please come to the front and I will pray for you." When he came off stage he could not understand why the rest of us were doubled over with laughter. We can all say things wrong! This experience didn't put him off speaking in public though as he has gone on to be a pastor of a large church.

My husband also was not put off by his first gaffe and has become an experienced speaker over the years. However, recently he made another mistake when he was speaking at a large church in Bristol. He told the audience that we should watch the video screen as we were going to watch a film on VD! Amidst the laughter that followed he had to explain that what he meant to say was: "we are going to watch a film on DVD"!! It just goes to show that no matter how experienced you are, you can still get it wrong!

**So don't worry if you make mistakes, everyone does! The key is to learn from them and not to give up!**

**Remember** everyone who succeeds has made many mistakes on their journey to success! The important difference is that when they came up against failure, they didn't give up, but allowed their mistakes to fuel their determination to continue to try.

# Which words do you find yourself saying?

~~I can't~~ I can
~~I think~~ I know
~~I'm afraid I can't attend~~ I can't attend
~~I'm only~~ I am

There is much power in the spoken word;
daily, speak out positive words.

When you need encouragement,
look at yourself in a mirror and
tell yourself,
## "I can do this!"

# Accelerator or Brake?

**D**on't allow what Ray and I call 'blockers' to destroy your faith and confidence.

Ray and I go swimming three times a week to try and keep ourselves fit and this exercise has taught me more than what you would expect. We've had people who come into the busy pool and despite the fact that they see you swimming up and down the pool doing your lengths, they will stand in the middle of the pool in your lane and talk with their friends. They block your way and make it much more difficult for you to achieve your aim.

Ever experienced a blocker? It may not be in a swimming pool, but could be in any avenue of life. It is someone who stands in your way and can think of every reason why you should not do what you feel you should do. I'm not talking about constructive criticism, this is always helpful, but I am talking about those people who through their own insecurity, lack of understanding or other motives try and talk you out of something that is a God-given vision or idea.

As leaders, this has happened to us many times! A number of years ago we brought to ngm what we thought was a God-given idea of helping the teenagers and those in their early twenties/thirties in our own local town. We live in a very quiet middle-class town not far from the bustling city centre of Bristol. During the day, our town is like any other town, but during Friday and Saturday nights it became a very different place. A lot of people did not go into the town centre late at night particularly at the weekends for fear of fights and vandalism.

Young people roamed the streets; often the shop windows were smashed through binge drinking and drug addiction. The police and the drug squads were often in our town during Friday and Saturday nights. It was not a safe place.

We felt a pull in our hearts to go and try and make a difference in our own town and suggested the idea first to our leadership team and then to ngm as a whole. The response from one person was to try and block the whole idea. We recognised that his concerns were coming from his lack of security and tried to put his fears to rest, but he was determined to try and come up with any and every excuse so that what we wanted to do would not happen. When you are a leader you want to hear how you can make things happen rather than every excuse possible as to why the idea would not work.

Eventually, we went ahead with the idea and it was the best work we had done for a long time. After many years of working on the streets from 8pm to 1.30am the police congratulated us on our work and told us the whole atmosphere in the area had changed.

> But as for you, be strong and do not give up, for your work will be rewarded
>
> 2 Chron 15:7

# You Lift My Head

*For years I've held my head in shame*
*No answer to my endless pain*
*I walk this desert desolate*
*I'm barren, empty, desperate*
*They say I'm drunk from red red wine*
*It's sorrow from a different vine*
*These tears I've cried the times I've died*
*So many prayers I've sighed*

*Every time I hear a voice from heaven say*
*My child you're beautiful*
*You gently wipe my falling tears away*
*When I feel you lift my head, I start to smile*
*Your peace like raindrops falls*
*Even though it's taken me a while*
*Father, please take my dreams, my all*

*Your breath of life has breathed on me*
*You've changed my life amazingly*
*My barrenness, now fertile land*
*A priceless gift from your own hand*
*I feel alive inside of me*
*Your love has made my life complete*
*I won't withhold your precious gift*
*I lay it at your feet*

© 2009 Ray Goudie & Phil Barlow
Song written for Hannah Franklin's album 'You are the song'.
Published by ngm/Intergritymusic 2009

*The Lord is my light and my*
*salvation – whom shall I fear?*
*The Lord is the stronghold of my*
*life – of whom shall I be afraid?*
*When evil men advance against me to*
*devour my flesh, when my enemies and my*
*foes attack me, they will stumble and fall.*
*Though an army besiege me, my heart will*
*not fear; though war break out against*
*me, even then will I be confident.*

Ps 27: 1-3

```
Our confidence comes
from his faithfulness!
```

Don't put your confidence in...

Money

Possessions

Your home

Your car

Your job

Fame

*All these things can let you down!
Instead, put your confidence in
the one who will never fail to be
at your side.*

# Confidence Builders

*I can do all things through him who strengthens me.*

Phil 4:13

*I am still confident of this: I will see the goodness of the Lord in the land of the living.*

Psalm 27:13

*Do not throw away your confidence; it will be richly rewarded. You need to persevere so that when you have done the will of God, you will receive what he has promised.*

Hebrews 10:35-36

*We are not of those who shrink back ... but are of those who believe*

Hebrews 10:39

*But as for you, be strong and do not give up, for your work will be rewarded.*

*We live by faith and not by sight*

*So we say with confidence, "The Lord is my helper; I will not be afraid. What can man do to me?"*

# Speak these words over your life and see the strength they bring

# Ruthless Trust

My precious and most amazing child, I want you
to know that I am your faithful friend. When life
is tough and hard, I won't run away, but I will be
with you at every turn. When all your resources
have disappeared, and you think the end is near,
don't worry I won't let you down. Even when you
cannot feel my presence and you feel all alone,
through the darkness I will be there for you.
Hold out your hand and remember the truth of
my words. I have promised never to leave you
nor to forsake you and the truth is, I never will!
It is impossible for me to let you down.

Trust me always!

# Don't Quit

*When things go wrong, as they sometimes will*
*When the road you're trudging seems all uphill*
*When the funds are low and the debts are high*
*And you want to smile, but you have to sigh*
*When care is pressing you down a bit*
*Rest if you must, but don't you quit.*

*Life is queer with its twists and turns*
*As every one of us sometimes learns*
*And many a fellow turns about*
*When he might have won, had he stuck it out.*
*Don't give up though the pace seems slow*
*You may succeed with another blow.*

*Often the goal is nearer than*
*It seems to a faint and faltering man;*
*Often the struggler has given up*
*When he might have captured the victor's cup;*
*And he learned too late when the night came down*
*How close he was to the golden crown.*

*Success is failure turned inside out*
*The silver tint of the clouds of doubt*
*And you never can tell how close you are*
*It may be near when it seems afar;*
*So stick to the fight when you're hardest hit*
*It's when things seem worst that you mustn't quit.*

Author Unknown

## Prescription

### Take these 4 pills everyday!

1. I can do it, I can make it, I will succeed!

2. There is nothing that God and I cannot achieve together!

3. I am special; there is no one like me!

4. I am an amazing creation; a person of much worth!

As you confess these truths each day, you will discover that they will find a lodging place in your heart that will lead to a new confident lifestyle.

# Like a little child

**E**ver watched a child trying to walk?  It's fascinating!
One day, after they have been crawling for some time,
they will try and pull themselves up by holding onto
the furniture.  When they eventually reach their full height they
will try to stand on their own, and that is when they fall to the
ground.  However, the remarkable thing is that no matter how
many times they fall, they will continue to climb up the furniture
until one day they will stand by themselves. When they do, they
will take a step forward and immediately they will be back on
their bottom again. But do they stay there?  No!  They get themselves back up on their feet and no matter how many times they
fall, they will continue to try because one day they will walk and
one day they will run!

   In life when difficulties and storms come there will be many
voices within and without telling you to give up.  At that point
when your confidence is low and when you have been knocked
down once more and you feel you just cannot do it anymore,
remember what you did as a child and don't stay on the floor.
Instead get back up on your feet because one day you will walk,
one day you will run!

Psalm 71:5

For you have been my hope, O Sovereign Lord, my
        confidence since my youth.

*Cast your cares on the Lord and he will sustain you; he will never let the righteous fall*

Psalm 55: 22

Our tears are always seen and our cries always heard

# Lord - hear my cry!

*Lord, everyone thinks I am doing okay.*
*They can't see the pain every day*
*They look on the outside and I say 'I'm alright'*
*Inside I am hurting, so dark with no light*
### *Lord, hear my cry!*

*Throughout every day the fears fill my eyes*
*I hide it inside surrounded by lies*
*A smile on my face that says it's okay*
*But my heart is torn with nothing to say*
### *Lord, hear my cry!*

*Harder and harder each day I'm alive*
*No hope for the 'moro, can I survive?*
*Who can I turn to, does anyone care?*
*Please give me some loving, give me my share*
### *Lord, hear my cry!*

Micah 7:7

But as for me, I watch in hope for the Lord, I
wait for God my Saviour; my God will hear me

49

# Keep smiling!

**D**uring the 80s our band, Heartbeat, were asked to go on a programme on BBC2. It was a new innovative programme about different faiths. The idea was to explore different faiths by taking one young person each programme and ask them about their faith in detail. They filmed us at one of our gigs as well as in one of our team worship times. Ray and I asked Sue Rinaldi, who was our lead singer at the time, if she would be the person who was put in the spotlight to answer the questions on our faith. She agreed and although we had not been given the questions from the BBC we knew the kind of questions they would ask. We trained Sue in how she should answer and also got her to contact some of our friends who were theologians and ask them how they would answer these kinds of questions.

The day finally came when Ray and Sue had to travel to Northern Ireland where this part of the show was being filmed. Sue was placed in the middle of a circle of young people whose remit was to ask their questions as aggressively as possible. We had soaked the programme in prayer and though the barrage of heated questions was very difficult, Sue kept going and answered each question with a smile. During each break Ray and Sue would confer as to how to answer. Sue was a star and came across really well. We were so proud of her. Throughout it all she never stopped smiling!

After the show we received hundreds of letters from people asking how to find God and a dynamic church. Throughout these letters a question kept appearing; they wanted to know how Sue managed to keep smiling when the questions were being asked with such antagonism. Sue explained that when she's nervous she always smiles! Sue didn't appear nervous at all; her smile gave her an air of confidence.

Try smiling; you may still feel nervous and under-confident inside, but smile lots and no-one will know!

*Laughter is one of the greatest releases of stress; laugh a lot it will help you through the toughest of times.*

I arrived in the USA with two friends, Zoe Wickham and Carey Robson to meet Joyce Meyer and attend her conference in Detriot. As we arrived at the immigration point, I was questioned as to why I wanted entry into the USA. I explained that I and my two friends were attending a conference. The man then questioned me very closely about the conference and was I absolutely sure I was coming into the country to attend a Joyce Meyer conference. I told him I was meeting her personally and that I had been in touch directly with her husband. He continued to question me with a straight face and I was beginning to feel that he didn't believe me and was not going to let me into the country. Eventually he told me that his wife was a fan of Joyce Meyer and that he had asked me all these questions because he wanted to pass the information on to his wife. Phew! My confidence returned!

A few days later we were visiting a restaurant and ordered our meals together with a glass of wine. The waitress immediately looked at all three of us and asked for our ID! I thought she was joking! My two companions are in their 30's and it's been a long time since I had my 21st! I laughed and she said, "I am not joking. I need each person's ID to check you are over 21." I told her, "This is the best restaurant in the world! That's the best compliment I have had in years - I will be back!" It's amazing how a compliment can give you increased confidence. We laughed about this for weeks!

# You've got to Laugh!

**R**ay and I recently had the privilege of meeting and getting to know a man who is a personal chaplain to the Queen. He came to our ngm offices because he wanted to find out more about our work. He is a very interesting and intriguing man and we got on like a house on fire! At the end of our conversation, he and Ray swopped personal phone numbers and then he left. Later on that day, Ray was at the hairdressers when he had a phone call from the same man asking if he could meet Ray again. He was in the High street of our town, just further up the road. So Ray went to meet him. I was to meet Ray at the hairdressers but of course when I arrived to pick him up in our car, he had gone. The hairdresser told me that Ray had gone to meet the Queen's personal chaplain. I explained that this could not be right as we had met him that morning. He said with a shrug, "Oh I don't know then, maybe he has gone to meet the Queen!" I laughed and went looking for Ray! I found him further up the High Street with our new friend. He told me to go on home and he would get dropped off later. I went to our local supermarket which was on the way home.

The first thing I saw when I arrived back at our home was that Ray was sitting in a vehicle outside our house talking to the Queen's personal chaplain and his assistant. I debated with myself, shall I go and say hello, knowing that I would have to invite him and his assistant into our home or should I just leave it and check the house first. I couldn't remember how I had left the house that morning and after all this was a personal chaplain to the Queen! So, I went into the house and quickly tidied it up just in case Ray decided to ask him in. I put all the rubbish I could find into the utility room at the back door and looked around the lounge and thought it look reasonable. I had just convinced myself that Ray would not invite him to come in, when I heard the door open! I went to invite them in, but then realised that Ray was bringing them in through the back door, past all the rubbish I had put there, past all the dirty washing and the ironing into the kitchen! This is the Queen's personal chaplain and Ray brought him in through the back door! I could not believe it – I mean what is it about men?!!

I quickly ushered them into the lounge praying that as they passed all the mess that they had temporarily lost their ability to see! After providing them with a drink, I sat in the lounge congratulating myself that I had checked the house before Ray brought them in, when all of a sudden, my eyes were opened! I could not believe it! How did I miss them? Right next to the Queen's personal chaplain drying over the radiator were two pairs of Ray's underpants!

Remember when things go wrong that it's not always possible to get everything right all of the time!

# LOL

Seen on church notice boards and information sheets:

THE FASTING & PRAYER CONFERENCE INCLUDES MEALS.

LOW SELF ESTEEM SUPPORT GROUP WILL MEET THURSDAY AT 7 PM. PLEASE USE BACK DOOR.

THE PEACEMAKING MEETING SCHEDULED FOR TODAY HAS BEEN CANCELLED DUE TO A CONFLICT.

The Rector will preach his farewell message after which the choir will sing: 'Break Forth Into Joy.'

LADIES, DON'T FORGET THE RUMMAGE SALE. IT'S A CHANCE TO GET RID OF THOSE THINGS NOT WORTH KEEPING AROUND THE HOUSE. BRING YOUR HUSBANDS.

Remember in prayer the many who are sick of our community. Smile at someone who is hard to love. Say 'Hell' to someone who doesn't care much about you.

The church will host an evening of fine dining, super entertainment and gracious hostility.

This evening at 7 PM there will be hymn singing in the park across from the Church. Bring a blanket and come prepared to sin.

# Superwoman

I was feeling particularly low one day, feeling that I was a failure! As usual when I feel like this I talk to God about it. I had just driven my son to school and on the way back I shared my feelings with God. I told him, "Lord I feel such a failure!" I had got annoyed with my son before he went to school and shouted at him. Although I had sorted it out with him before I drove him to school it still left me with even more feelings of failure. In the car on the way home from Aidan's school, I told God I felt a failure as a Mum never mind everything else. As the tears fell, God spoke to me and said, "Nancy you are not a failure, in fact let me tell you who you are - you are Superwoman! Why? Because you have the Almighty God living inside of you! I am the God who created the universe! I am the God of the impossible! I am able to do anything and everything!" God reminded me that I was clothed with Jesus and that the Bible tells me that although Jesus did powerful, amazing miracles throughout his life here on earth, we can see even greater things happen through us! Wow! I began to believe it! God said to me, "So who are you?" I laughed and said, "Lord I am superwoman!" The Lord said "I cannot hear you. Let me hear you shout it out!" God had me shouting it loudly in the car again and again; "I am superwoman!"

Today no matter how you are feeling, remember you are not a failure! Indeed if God lives in you, then you have the amazing creator of the universe living inside of you and you are indeed Superwoman/man! Come on, let me hear you shout it out…

# I
# AM
# SUPER-
# WOMAN!
## (OR MAN!)

# JOY is...

energising

freeing          contagious

beautiful

precious  overwhelming

a gift  all powerful

anti-aging

boundless

all conquering

healthy

good for body, soul and spirit

breathtaking

free

a stress buster

a visitor worth       victorious
inviting again

Is Jesus!

# Ten top tips

**1** Smile, smile, smile, smile, smile, smile, smile, smile, smile. Smiling relaxes your body!

**2** Remember failures are stepping stones to getting it right. So pick yourself up and keep going!

**3** Push through any fear; when you speak, speak clearly believing that your contribution to the conversation is important!

**5** Look into the eyes of each person you meet; avoiding their eyes makes you appear under confident.

**4** Know that you are capable of doing far more than you can dream or even imagine.

**6** Don't live in the pocket of someone who constantly puts you down, criticises you and tells you that you are no good. Instead surround yourself with encouraging, positive people!

**8** Laugh at yourself when things go wrong.

**7** Be prepared to learn from others. Listen to helpful advice.

**9** Have a positive outlook on life; encourage others and you will encourage yourself too.

**10** Never be half-hearted; give all you have to give.

# I Hope to Pass

I heard a story about two boys, one was called Cecil and one was called Fred. Cecil was very clever and could be described as a pile of books on two legs! He was always on time for his lectures and was never without a large amount of books in his hands. Fred on the other hand was always running late, never seemed to have the right books for the right lecture and was always getting into trouble from his tutors. At the end of their course, both were facing the same exams and both were asked if they thought they would do well. Cecil's reply was, 'I hope to pass' When Fred was asked he also said, 'I hope to pass'. Both had answered with the same words, however the meaning was completely different. When Cecil had given his reply the word 'hope' meant he had overwhelming confidence. On the other hand when Fred said 'I hope to pass' he meant he was hoping against hope that somehow he would pass his exams.

We can all have Cecil's kind of hope and have overwhelming confidence in the fact that with God we can face whatever the future holds.

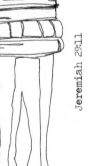

> For I know the plans I have for you, declares the Lord, plans to prosper you and not to harm you, plans to give you hope and a future.
>
> Jeremiah 29:11

# Can we build it?

## Yes we can!

Write down a compliment someone has given you!

Write down a success you have achieved - and remember it more than any failures.

Let any failure make you stronger. Write down what went wrong and how you can avoid that in future.

Write down one encouraging verse and memorise it.

You have been created with many qualities. Write down at least one.

Look at someone who appears to be confident and write down something you can learn from them.

# The Lion Roars

I loved the film 'Prince Caspian' and particularly loved the bit where little Lucy is standing at the edge of a bridge in front of the enemy. The enemy is huge and has many weapons. They look barbaric and fierce and the only person trying to stop them crossing this bridge is this cute, little girl. You would have thought that she would have been frightened, but she looks quietly confident even although from the outside looking in it looks like this little girl is about to be annihilated! It seems quite pathetic when she produces her little dagger. Her situation looks overwhelming! However, when the enemy charges towards her, Aslan, the lion, appears beside her and roars. The enemy is defeated even before they get half way across the bridge. No wonder Lucy was confident! She knew she was not alone.

**Always remember we can be confident when we have the Lion of Judah right beside us! Whatever you face, know that you and God can face it together!**

*The Lord's unfailing love surrounds the one who trusts in him.*

*I will never leave you nor will I forsake you.*

Psalms 32:10

Deut 31:8

# When I say... You say...

I'm afraid ...        I am there for you!

I'm full of fear      My love will chase all
and anxiety ...        your fears away!

It's impossible ...   I am the God of the impossible

I'm a failure ...     You are a success!

I am weak ...         You are strong

I have                You are wonderful and have many
nothing to give ...    amazing qualities and gifts to share!

I just can't do it! ...  You can do all things through
                       me and my strength.

I have no-one
to help ...           I am your constant helper.

I am not accepted ... I always welcome and accept you!

I'm rubbish ...       There is no one more pre-
                       cious than you!

I am small and        You are very significant, you
insignificant ...      are special and you are mine!

                      You are my amazing child, my
                      glorious one. You delight my
I am not loved ...     heart and fill me with overflow-
                      ing joy. I will always love you.

## Through me and my love you can have confidence to do all things.

# Remember Remember

## Feeling defeated?
*Remember that we are more than
conquerors through him who loved us!*

Romans 8:37

## Feeling worried?
*Remember, don't worry about anything
instead pray about everything.*

Phil 4:6

## Feeling small?
*Remember we serve the God of the Universe! He
made the stars in the sky! He can hold the oceans
in the palm of his hand. We may be small but
he is HUGE and he can do all things!*

Is 40:12&15

## Feeling lonely?
*Remember God is with you every moment of every day
and he promises that he will never leave nor forsake you.*

Deut 31:8

## Feeling anxious?
*Remember the Lord wants us to cast
all our anxiety on to Him.*

1 Peter 5:7

## Feeling afraid?
*Remember that God has commanded his
angels to guard you in all your ways.*

Psalm 91:9–12

# Feeling troubled?

*Remember, don't let your heart be troubled.*
*Trust in God…*

John 14:1

# Feeling dismayed?

*Remember our God can change circumstances even if*
*it seems impossible – He is the God of the impossible!*

Jer 32:26

# Feeling a failure?

*Remember God can change every defeat into a victory!  It*
*says in the Bible that in ALL things God works for the good*
*of those who love him.  Wow!  Allow him to work in your*
*circumstances and look for the good that God will bring.*

Romans 8:28

# Feeling fearful?

*Remember God is our refuge and strength, an*
*ever present help in trouble.  The mighty God of*
*the universe is with you every moment. Therefore,*
*do not to fear even if the worst happens!*

Ps 46:1-3

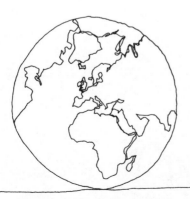

Nothing will seem as
difficult when He holds
your hand

# I will wait for Him

Lamentations 3: 19–24

*I remember my affliction and my wandering, the bitterness and the gall. I remember them well, and my soul is downcast within me. Yet, this I call to mind and therefore I have hope: because of the Lord's great love we are not consumed, for his compassions never fail. They are new every morning; great is your faithfulness. I will say to myself, "The Lord is my portion therefore I will wait for him."*

Lord, I remember the heartache, the hurt, the pain, the fear! I remember them well; the rejection, the lies spoken against us, the friendships lost, the pain of people's words. I remember them all too well and my heart breaks and my spirit is down within me. YET, I call to mind, I choose to call to mind that your love is great for me and mine! In this I have hope, a glimmer of hope appears and as I put my faith in that hope, things appear differently. Because of your great overwhelming love for me and mine, we are not consumed, we are not overcome by sorrow, for your compassions **never** fail me. They are new, fresh, wonderfully available every morning - for great, so wonderfully great is your faithfulness. You cannot be faithless; you continue to be faithful to me/mine every day. **I will say to myself**, I will tell my innermost being, The Lord is my portion, therefore no matter how long it takes, I will wait for him.

Thank you Lord!

This paraphrase of Lamentations 3:19-24 was written during a time of pain and suffering; when Nancy's husband Ray experienced two years of ill health and burnout and where pressures seemed to soar to the highest heights. To read the whole story - see Nancy's book called 'Treasures of Darkness' - www.nancygoudie.com

# Jackie Doherty ∧ In Confidence‼

*(handwritten above line: "not")*

**I** understand only too well the issue of confidence. There can be many reasons why a person has a lack of confidence, real or imagined.

On the surface, most people would describe me as a confident person, certainly I had never experienced any confidence issues…that was, at least, until a few years ago. One day I opened the newspapers and found not only had they reported a story about my son Peter, but lots of it was untrue. Since that time I have read many articles in the papers and seen news items online written about me or members of my family; written by people who did not know me, words written in black and white which were sometimes completely untrue! I feel grossly misrepresented when strangers and family alike tell me what has been written about me; lies such as: I have been treated for breast cancer, or I have been standing outside Pentonville prison pleading to get in to see Peter.

The list is a long one, almost as long as the inaccuracies. One report was that I had fled from Devon to be at his bedside as he was in a drug-induced sleep. The truth was he was playing a gig and I went there to watch him! I once read in the papers that Peter had had to be resuscitated on stage the previous night. I called his then manager and was surprised when Peter answered the phone. I burst out crying whilst trying to explain to Peter what I had read! He laughed out loud and told me to stop reading the tabloids. The story was completely untrue! There have been many stories and many lies, too many to document.

Due to the pressure of having a child (even though the child was a man!) always in the papers or on television, the media charting his every move and reporting upon it, I often felt a severe lack of confidence! I would find it hard to leave the house, or to go to work, or even to talk with my neighbours…but I did leave the house! I never missed a day of work and yes, I even talked with my neighbours… not because of anything in me but because of everything in Him, I was able to put on my lipstick, hold my head high and walk through the raging storm.

My storm rages on but I know I don't walk through it alone. God never promised us an easy life but He absolutely promises to be with us. One of my favourite verses in the Bible about confidence is this:-

Isaiah 30:15*

'In quietness and confidence shall be your strength'*

# confidence

*How can I put on this lipstick!*
*How can I walk through the door?*
*How can I chat with my neighbours,*
*with whom I've oft chatted before.*

*Why is my heart all a tremble!*
*Why is my spirit cast down?*
*Why can't I just lift my head up?*
*Why is my smile now a frown?*

*I'll bring it to God straight away*
*in prayer, in faith, in this hour.*
*My part is only to call Him,*
*Then to trust upon His healing power.*

# Through It All

Through all the hardship, through all the pain,
through all the worry, through all the strain.
Through all the stress, through all the tears,
through all the heartache and through all the fears.

**You have been my constant strength and support.**

Though friends may wound me and pain abounds
There's just one thing that I have found
When in the midst of a stormy sea
You never left or deserted me.

**You have been my constant strength and support.**

Through everything, one thing is my gain
Through everything, through all the shame
I've learned to trust, I've learned to praise
I've learned to walk in all your ways.

# Do not merely listen to the word...

## DO WHAT IT SAYS!

"Everyone who hears these words of mine and puts them into practice is like a wise man who built his house on the rock. The rain came down, the streams rose, and the winds blew and beat against that house; yet it did not fall, because it had its foundation on the rock. But everyone who hears these words of mine and does not put them into practice is like a foolish man who built his house on sand. The rain came down, the streams rose, and the winds blew and beat against that house and it fell with a great crash."

Jesus

Build on a good foundation and you will have confidence even in the midst of a storm

God's never ending, unfailing love
for you!

Though the mountains be shaken
and the hills be removed, yet my
unfailing love for you will not be
shaken nor my covenant of peace
be removed

Isaiah 54:10

Always know that you are God's
Beloved! His unfailing love for you
will never end.

# I Dance with Delight!

What joy; what grace fills my heart when I look at you.  You are glorious, beautiful and amazing!  I have loved you from the beginning and covered you with my joy.  If you were to look the world over, you would not find a love like mine!  There is no one who loves you more than me.  When I first saw you, my heart exploded with joy and delight.  I loved you from before time began and covered you with my grace.  My favour was poured out upon you and I, throughout all your days, have danced with delight over you. My heart aches with love for you and whether you know it or not, I have held you in my arms even from before you were born and I will do forever and ever!

Real confidence comes from knowing God's overwhelming, unconditional, amazing love for us

# What is life?

Life is sacred

Life is precious

Life is special

Life is unique

Life is a gift

Life is to be enjoyed

Life is beautiful

Life is hard

Life is a challenge

Life is colourful

Life is difficult

Jesus said,
*"I have come that you may have
life and have it to the full."*

Enjoy life in all its colour, beauty and fullness.
Life may suck at times and everything may go wrong,
but remember when it does not to throw away the beautiful, wonderful, amazing gift that God has given you!
Ask him to help you enjoy his gift of life to the full.

You only have one life,
let's live it to the best we can!

# Look up

*When all around crumbles and falls;*
*look up and trust in God.*

*When structures around seem flimsy and weak;*
*look up and trust in God.*

*When politicians, bankers and the economy let you down;*
*look up and trust in God.*

*When family and friends cannot provide what you need;*
*look up and trust in God.*

There is no one like our God!

He remains unshakable,
unchangeable in a shaky forever
changing world.

He remains faithful in a faithless
society.

He is everything he ever said he
was and always will be.

# Forgiven
## what an amazing word!

There are not many words in the English language that are as wonderful as the word 'Forgiven'! When you do something wrong, the guilt of what you have done remains with you, sometimes for the rest of your life whether you have said sorry or not! However, when the person you have wronged forgives you, not only is the guilt washed away, but it feels like you have had a bath on the inside. Forgiveness leads to a more whole and confident you!

## What an amazing experience it is to be forgiven!

**Those who have been forgiven much love much!**
**Those who have been forgiven little love little**
JESUS

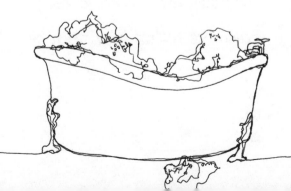

# If God stopped thinking of me, he would cease to exist

Angelus Silesius
15th century theologian


Are not five sparrows sold for two pennies? Yet not one of them is forgotten by God. Indeed the very hairs of your head are all numbered. Don't be afraid; you are worth more than many sparrows.

Jesus


## God is always thinking of us - Wow!

Trusting God becomes easy when we realise how much he loves us.

Ps 62:5-8

*Find rest O my soul in God alone;*
*my hope comes from him.*
*He alone is my rock and my salvation;*
*he is my fortress, I will not be shaken.*
*My Salvation and my honour depend on God;*
*he is my mighty rock, my refuge.*
*Trust in him at all times O people;*
*pour out your hearts to him*
*for God is our refuge.*

1 Cor 2:9

No eye has seen, no ear has heard, no mind has conceived what God has prepared for those who love him.

You cannot even begin to imagine or conceive the amazing future that is planned and purposed for you his glorious child!

**The truth is that the best is yet to come!**

# The Garden

I want you to come with me to a perfect place of peace and rest. Close your eyes to all around you and begin to imagine an amazing garden which is full of beauty and creativity.

As you begin to explore this garden you realise that you have never been anywhere so amazing before. There are huge trees which have been planted a long time ago and are bearing much fruit. There are thousands of shrubs and flowers which spread their fragrance and beauty abroad. You notice that there are some seedlings that have recently been tenderly planted. The grass is luscious and green; the whole place looks like no garden you have ever seen before. There are no weeds that you can see. There is a wonderful slow moving river which winds its way through the garden. The whole place is full of peace, joy and tranquillity.

As you explore the garden, the gardener approaches you and says, "I love to walk in this garden; it is so full of peace, beauty and promise." You ask him, "where is this place?" He looks straight at you and says, "This is the garden of your life. Do you not know how beautiful you are? Can you not see how wonderfully you have been created? You are this beautiful garden. Each time you say a kind word to someone, each time you do a good deed, each time you have a happy thought, every time you are selfless, I plant a seedling and over the years it grows and grows."

You are astonished at what you are hearing and say to the gardener, "But what about the times when I have been negative and hard? What about the times when I have been angry and annoyed? What about the times when I have uttered unkind words?" The gardener replies, "At times there are weeds, for every time you say an unkind word or think a negative thought a bitter root is planted. However, when you ask for forgiveness or extend forgiveness towards someone who has hurt you, I then pull out that weed of bitterness from your garden, but I don't just pull out that one, I pull out any other weeds that are there at the same time. You ask for forgiveness for one thing, but I forgive you for all you have done wrong. When you walk in forgiveness, you walk in beauty and peace. Look around you. This is a place of tranquillity. This is a place of colour and joy. This is the garden of your life.

This is you!"

This is you!

# Do you know?

- that you are special, one of a kind; there is no-one like you?

- that before you were born God loved you?

- that God chose you before the foundations of the world were put in place?

- that God shaped and formed you in the womb into the amazing person you are?

- that from your birth he called you by name?

- that you were never a mistake but that you were loved from the beginning

**Always remember you are special!**

On what
are you
basing your
confidence?

# Nancy Goudie's
## Spiritual Health Weekends

THREE EXCITING DAYS TO TRANSFORM YOUR WALK WITH GOD

## Would you like to be pampered physically and toned up spiritually?

## Nancy Goudie's Spiritual Health Weekends could be just the thing you are looking for!

Nancy Goudie runs weekend conferences at the end of January and the beginning of February each year at luxury four-star Marriot Hotels in Preston and Bristol. The weekend is for ladies of all ages. Come and enjoy the excellent food and leisure facilities (spa, steam room, sauna, fitness room and luxury pool) and also experience God through the inspirational teaching and creative spiritual exercises from Nancy. Special guests include some of the talented ngm artists. Each conference is booked well in advance so please book early to avoid disappointment.

This is a women's conference like no other!

For more information and booking details contact:

Zoe Wickham at ngm, Caedmon Complex, Bristol Road, Thornbury, Bristol BS35 3JA.

Tel: 01454 414880
Fax: 01454 414812
Email: zoewickham@ngm.org.uk
www.nancygoudie.com

# Other Books & Products
## By Nancy Goudie

### Spiritual Health Workout (£6.99)

This unique book is practical, accessible and fun to use and will help you exercise your faith muscles and tone up your heart for God. It is an excellent book for individuals and small groups.

*"The depth of Nancy's faith and spirituality are the genuine products of years of walking with the Lord and seeking to serve him – that's why I am recommending her writing to you"* – Steve Chalke, Oasis Trust.

### HOT Faith (£7.99)

If you want to find out about how ngm started or the amazing miracles that happened during their five year walk of faith to get their amazing missions and arts centre (Caedmon) then Nancy's book H.O.T. Faith (Hearing, Obeying, Trusting) is the book for you. It is a book filled with stories of faith exploits and will encourage you to walk by faith every day in life.

*"Whatever mountains you need to move, this remarkable book will build your faith and empower your prayers"*
Pete Greig (24/7 Prayer)

### Treasures of Darkness (£5.00)

This is a very naked and honest autobiographical account of a time when the world around Nancy started to collapse. Her husband Ray fell into a dark pit where he experienced ill health and burnout. At the same time God was taking their ministry, ngm, through a shift, which caused much pain and insecurity and led to many people eventually leaving. Pressures swept in like a storm leaving confusion and unanswered prayers. Nancy discovered that through this time there were 'treasures of darkness and riches hidden in a secret place' (Isaiah 45:3).

The Beloved (£5.00 Hardback)

This is a collection of real stories, poems, wise words, meditations and huge encouragement to know that you are God's beloved child. Any time you are feeling down, unloved, criticised or critical of yourself and life hits you hard, then pick up this book and flick through its pages. Each page is designed to bring you words of encouragement, hope and love.

Spiritual Health Magazines (£1.00)

Filled with stories, advice, tips and interesting articles – a great glossy magazine to brighten up your day!

Bible Reading Planners (50p)

A superb way of systematically reading through the Bible in one or two years.

Smile (£8.00 Meditation CD)

If you are feeling the daily stresses of life, the busyness of work, the pressures of family or just need some soothing for your soul, then this recording is for you.

**Peace Like a River** (£8.00 Meditation CD)
If you have ever experienced stress, carried worries, fought fears or are just looking for an oasis in your busy life – then this CD is for you. This recording will take you to a place of tranquillity where peace love and grace are yours in abundance. Use this CD daily and you will find peace like a river flowing through your soul.

**A God Encounter** (£5.00 Meditation CD)
A unique meditative worship experience which will transport you to the very throne room of God.

**Journey to the Cross** (£5.00 Meditation CD)
A powerful CD that will take you to the foot of the cross to experience Christ's death, and impact you with the amazing love of God.

All the above products are available direct from:
    ngm, Caedmon Complex, Bristol Road,
    Thornbury, Bristol, UK. BS35 3JA.
    Tel: +44 (0)1454 414880

**www.ngm.org.uk**
**www.nancygoudie.com**
**All books are also available on Amazon.co.uk**

You can contact Nancy at the above address, or at:
nancy@nancygoudie.com.

illustration

<u>Contact</u> me if you like:

Charlotte@
charlottecookeillustration.com
or
07793239661

www.charlottecookeillustration.com